# Jane Austen
## Illustrated Quotations

# Jane Austen
## Illustrated Quotations

Bodleian Library
UNIVERSITY OF OXFORD

'I do not want people
to be very agreeable,
as it saves me the
trouble of liking
them a great deal.'

*Letter to Cassandra Austen on Christmas Eve, 1798*

'...it is better to know as little as possible of the defects of the person with whom you are about to pass your life.'

*Charlotte Lucas to Elizabeth Bennet,* Pride and Prejudice

'How horrible it is to have so many people killed! And what a blessing that one cares for none of them!'

*Letter to Cassandra Austen on the Peninsular War, 31 May 1811*

'I have now attained the true art of letter-writing, which we are always told, is to express on paper exactly what one would say to the same person by word of mouth.'

*Letter to Cassandra Austen, 3 January 1801*

'We are to have a tiny party here tonight. I hate tiny parties, they force one into constant exertion.'

*Letter to Cassandra Austen, 21 May 1801*

'We have been exceedingly busy ever since you went away. In the first place we have had to rejoice two or three times every day at your having such very delightful weather for the whole of your journey...'

*Letter to Cassandra Austen, 25 October 1800*

Illustration from *The World in Miniature* edited by W.H. Pyne, London, 1827.

'The pleasures of friendship, of unreserved conversation, of similarity of taste and opinions, will make good amends for orange wine.'

*Letter to Cassandra Austen, 20 June 1808*

'You express so little anxiety
about my being murdered
under Ash Park Copse by
Mrs Hulbert's servant,
that I have a great mind
not to tell you whether
I was or not.'

*Letter to Cassandra Austen, 8 January 1799*

'By the bye, as I must leave off being young, I find many *douceurs* in being a sort of *chaperon*, for I am put on the sofa near the fire and can drink as much wine as I like.'

*Letter to Cassandra Austen, 6 November 1813*

Evening dress from Ackermann's
*Repository*, London, 1819.

'I believe I drank too much
wine last night at Hurstbourne;
I know not how else to account
for the shaking of my hand to-day.
You will kindly make allowance
therefore for any indistinctness
of writing, by attributing it to
this venial error.'

*Letter to Cassandra Austen, 20 November 1800*

'Walter Scott has no business
to write novels, especially good
ones. It is not fair. He has fame
and profit enough as a poet, and
should not be taking the bread
out of other people's mouths.
I do not like him, and do not
mean to like *Waverley* if I can
help it, but fear I must.'

*Letter to Anna Austen Lefroy, 28 September 1814*

Portrait of Sir Walter Scott
by William Nicholson, 1817.

'I could no more write a romance than an epic poem. I could not sit seriously down to write a serious romance under any other motive than to save my life; and if it were indispensable for me to keep it up and never relax into laughing at myself or other people, I am sure I should be hung before I had finished the first chapter. No, I must keep to my own style and go on in my own way; and though I may never succeed again in that, I am convinced that I should totally fail in any other.'

*Letter to James Stanier Clarke, 1 April 1816*

Early editions of *Sense and Sensibility*, *Pride and Prejudice*, *Mansfield Park*, *Emma* and *Northanger Abbey and Persuasion* by Jane Austen.

'Single women have a dreadful propensity for being poor, which is one very strong argument in favour of matrimony.'

*Letter to Fanny Knight, 13 March 1817*

'Happiness in marriage is entirely a matter of chance.'

*Charlotte Lucas to Elizabeth Bennet,* Pride and Prejudice

'I give you joy of our new nephew, and hope if he ever comes to be hanged it will not be till we are too old to care about it.'

*Letter to Cassandra Austen on the birth of a son to one of their sisters-in-law, 25 April 1811*

'Vanity and pride are different things, though the words are often used synonymously. A person may be proud without being vain. Pride relates more to our opinion of ourselves; vanity, to what we would have others think of us.'

*Mary Bennet*, Pride and Prejudice

'How little of permanent happiness could belong to a couple who were only brought together because their passions were stronger than their virtue.'

*Pride and Prejudice*

*Harmony before Matrimony* by James Gillray, 1805.

'The more I know of the world, the more I am convinced that I shall never see a man whom I can really love.'

*Marianne Dashwood*, Sense and Sensibility

'There is something so amiable in the prejudices of a young mind, that one is sorry to see them give way to the reception of more general opinions.'

*Colonel Brandon*, Sense and Sensibility

French fashion plate, autumn 1795.

Aout. 1792.

'It sometimes happens, that a woman is handsomer at twenty-nine than she was ten years before.'

*Persuasion*

Portrait of Emma Jane Hodges by Charles Howard Hodges, *c.*1810.

'Our ball was rather more amusing than I expected...The melancholy part was, to see so many dozen young women standing by without partners, and each of them with two ugly naked shoulders! It was the same room in which we danced fifteen years ago! I thought it all over, and in spite of the shame of being so much older, felt with thankfulness that I was quite as happy now as then.'

*Letter to Cassandra Austen, 9 December 1808*

'There are such beings in the world – perhaps one in a thousand – as the creature you and I should think perfection; where grace and spirit are united to worth, where the manners are equal to the heart and understanding; but such a person may not come in your way, or, if he does, he may not be the eldest son of a man of fortune, the near relation of your particular friend, and belonging to your own county.'

*Letter to Fanny Knight, 18 November 1814*

'One half of the world cannot understand the pleasures of the other.'

*Emma Woodhouse to her father*, Emma

'There is nothing like staying at home for real comfort.'

*Mrs Elton*, Emma

'Poor woman!
how can she honestly
be breeding again?'

*Letter to Cassandra Austen, 1 October 1808*

*The Progress of Female Virtue*, Antoine
Cardon after Maria Cosway, 1800.

'Surprizes are foolish things. The pleasure is not enhanced, and the inconvenience is often considerable.'

*Mr Knightley*, Emma

*Company shocked at a Lady getting up to Ring the Bell* by James Gillray, 1804.

'Vanity working on a weak head, produces every sort of mischief.'

*Mr Knightley,* Emma

*Monstrosities of 1819* by George Cruikshank.

'I am almost afraid to tell you how my Irish friend and I behaved. Imagine to yourself everything most profligate and shocking in the way of dancing and sitting down together.'

*Letter to Cassandra Austen, 9 January 1796*

*Vis à vis accidents in Quadrille dancing,*
after George Cruikshank, 1817.

'Seldom, very seldom, does complete truth belong to any human disclosure; seldom can it happen that something is not a little disguised, or a little mistaken.'

*Emma*

Presentation copy of *Emma* sent to the Prince Regent by Jane Austen in 1815.

'Dress is at all times a
frivolous distinction,
and excessive solicitude
about it often destroys
its own aim.'

*Northanger Abbey*

*How to attract public notice* by George Cruikshank, 1818.

'It would be mortifying to the feelings of many ladies, could they be made to understand how little the heart of man is affected by what is costly or new in their attire.'

*Northanger Abbey*

'Next week (I) shall begin my operations on my hat, on which you know my principal hopes of happiness depend.'

*Letter to Cassandra Austen, 27 October 1798*

'I learnt from Mrs Tickars's young lady, to my high amusement, that the stays now are not made to force the bosom up at all; *that* was a very unbecoming, unnatural fashion.'

*Letter to Cassandra Austen, 15 September 1813*

*Progress of the Toilet – The Stays* by James Gillray, 1818.

GUILLAUMOT FILS. Sc.

'Friendship is certainly the finest balm for the pangs of disappointed love.'

*Northanger Abbey*

'The person, be it gentleman or lady, who has not pleasure in a good novel, must be intolerably stupid.'

*Henry Tilney*, Northanger Abbey

'But there certainly are not so many men of large fortune in the world as there are pretty women to deserve them.'

*Mansfield Park*

Detail from *The Third Tour of Dr Syntax, in Search of a Wife* 1821), by William Combe, illustrated by Thomas Rowlandson.

'A large income is the
best recipe for happiness
I ever heard of.'

*Mary Crawford*, Mansfield Park

*The Successful Fortune Hunter* by Thomas Rowlandson, 1812

Just
Published

'Give a girl an education, and introduce her properly into the world, and ten to one but she has the means of settling well, without farther expense to anybody.'

*Mrs Norris*, Mansfield Park

'A woman, especially if she has the misfortune of knowing anything, should conceal it as well as she can.'

*Northanger Abbey*

'Selfishness must always be forgiven, you know, because there is no hope of a cure.'

*Mary Crawford*, Mansfield Park

*The Necessary Qualifications of a Man of Fashion* by Daniel Thomas Egerton, 1823.

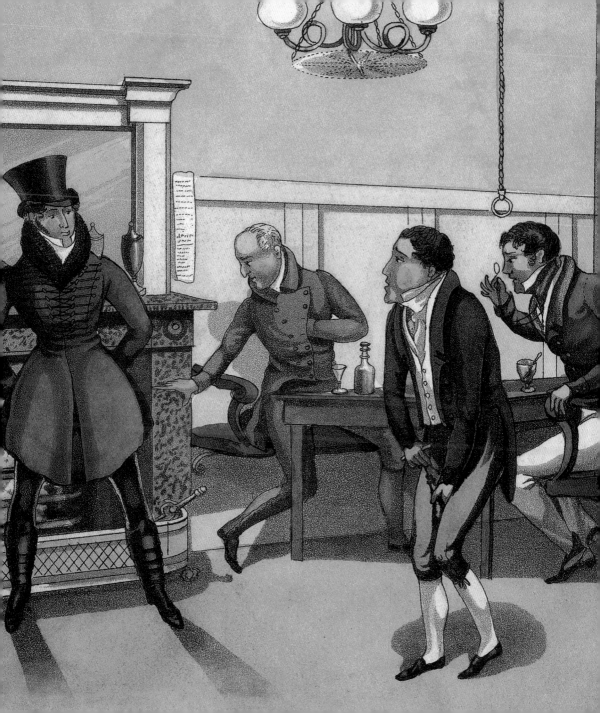

'What dreadful hot weather
we have! It keeps one in a
continual state of inelegance.'

*Letter to Cassandra Austen, 18 September 1796*

*A Summer Day* by John Sell Cotman *c.*1827.

'We do not look in
our great cities for
our best morality.'

*Edmund Bertram*, Mansfield Park

'It is a lovely night, and they are much to be pitied who have not… been given a taste for Nature in early life. They lose a great deal.'

*Edmund Bertram to Fanny Price*, Mansfield Park

'Open carriages are nasty things. A clean gown is not five minutes wear in them. You are splashed getting in and getting out; and the wind takes your hair and your bonnet in every direction. I hate an open carriage myself.'

*Mrs Allen*, Northanger Abbey

Illustration from Nikolaus Heideloff's *Gallery of Fashion*, vol. I, August 1794.

'To be fond of dancing
was a certain step
towards falling in love.'

*Pride and Prejudice*

'…but you know we must marry. – I could do very well single for my own part – A little company, and a pleasant ball now and then, would be enough for me, if one could be young for ever, but my Father cannot provide for us, and it is very bad to grow old and be poor and laughed at.'

*Elizabeth Watson*, The Watsons

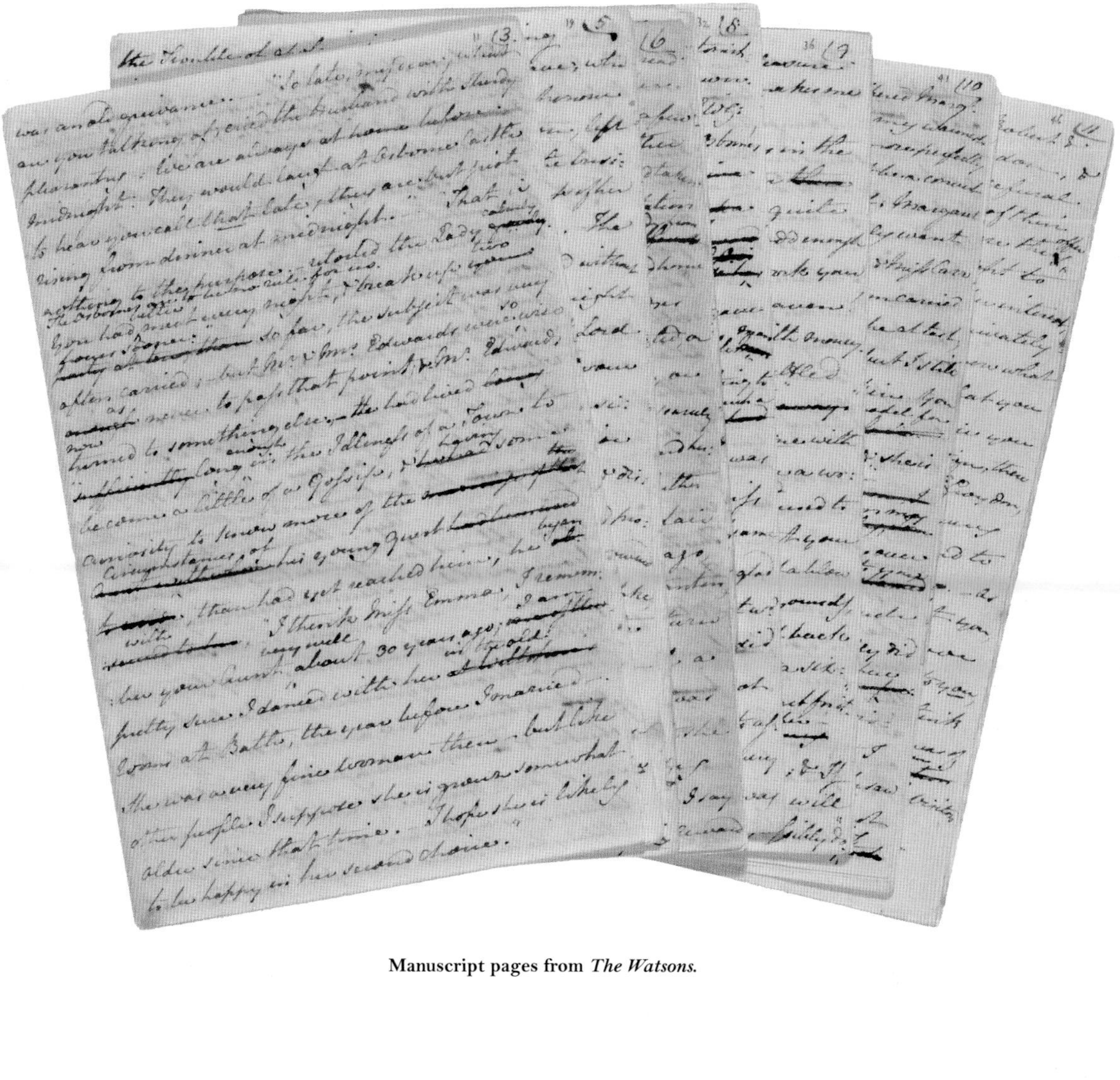

Manuscript pages from *The Watsons.*

'…to pursue a man merely for the sake of situation — is a sort of thing that shocks me; I cannot understand it. Poverty is a great evil, but to a woman of education and feeling it ought not, it cannot be the greatest. — I would rather be a teacher at a school (and I can think of nothing worse) than marry a man I did not like.'

*Emma Watson*, The Watsons

'Here I am once more in this scene of dissipation and vice, and I begin to find already my morals corrupted.'

*Letter to Cassandra Austen (on arrival in London), 23 August 1796*

'Men have had every advantage of us in telling their own story. Education has been theirs in so much higher a degree; the pen has been in their hands. I will not allow books to prove any thing.'

*Anne Elliot*, Persuasion

'...the first view of Bath in fine weather does not answer my expectations; I think I see more distinctly through rain. The sun was got behind everything, and the appearance of the place from the top of Kingsdown was all vapour, shadow, smoke and confusion.'

*Letter to Cassandra Austen, 5 May 1801*

*A View of Bath, c.1750.*

'The walk was very beautiful as my companion agreed, whenever I made the observation – And so our friendship ended, for the Chamberlaynes leave Bath in a day or two.'

*Letter to Cassandra Austen, 27 May 1801*

*North Parade, Bath*, by Humphry Repton, 1784.

'"Oh! It is only a novel!"…only some work in which the greatest powers of the mind are displayed, in which the most thorough knowledge of human nature, the happiest delineation of its varieties, the liveliest effusions of wit and humour, are conveyed to the world in the best-chosen language.'

*Northanger Abbey*

# Frederic & Elfrida

## a novel.

## Chapter the First.

The Uncle of Elfrida was the
Father
~~Mother~~ of Frederic; in other words, they
were first cousins by the Father's side.

Being both born in one day & both
brought up at one school, it was not
wonderfull that they should look on each
other with something more than bare po
:lite*ness. They loved with mutual sin:
:cerity but were both determined not to
transgress the rules of Propriety by owning
their attachment, either to the object beloved, or
to any one else.

## PICTURE CREDITS

2. New York Public Library, Jerome Robbins Dance Division

5. Oxford, Bodleian Library, Rec. e.115

6. Oxford, Bodleian Library, John Johnson Collection, Trade in Prints and Scraps 9 (9)

9. Oxford, Bodleian Library, 22871 c.9

11. Oxford, Bodleian Library, 8° D 432 BS. England, Scotland and Ireland, Vol 1, p. 100

12. Yale Center for British Art, Paul Mellon Collection

15. Houghton Library, Harvard University

16. Private Collection / The Stapleton Collection / Bridgeman Images

19. Oxford, Bodleian Library, Vet. A5 e.6138/3

20. Los Angeles County Museum of Art, Gift of Charles LeMaire (M.83.161.205)

22. Private collection

24. Library of Congress, Prints and Photographs Collection

27. Oxford, Bodleian Library, Dunston B 124; Arch. AA e.23; Dunston B 120; Dunston B 119; Dunston B 121

28. Yale Center for British Art, Paul Mellon Collection

31. National Gallery of Art, Washington, Paul Mellon Collection, 1983.1.43

32. Yale Center for British Art, Paul Mellon Collection

35. Yale University Art Gallery

36. Everett Historical / Shutterstock

39. National Gallery of Art, Washington, Given in memory of Governor Alvan T. Fuller by The Fuller Foundation, Inc., 1961.2.2

41. Metropolitan Museum of Art, Costume Institute Fashion Plates

43. Everett Art / Shutterstock

44. New York Public Library, Jerome Robbins Dance Division

47. Jane Austen's House Museum

49. Yale Center for British Art, Paul Mellon Collection

50. Jane Austen's House Museum

53. Yale University Art Gallery

54. Oxford, Bodleian Library, John Johnson Collection, Fashion folder 3 (12)

57. Everett Art / Shutterstock

58. New York Public Library, Jerome Robbins Dance Division

61. Royal Collection Trust / © Her Majesty Queen Elizabeth II 2016

62. Oxford, Bodleian Library, John Johnson Collection, Trade in Prints and Scraps 18 (48a)

65. Private Collection / Bridgeman Images

67. Los Angeles County Museum of Art, Gift of Charles LeMaire (M.83.161.188)

69. © The British Library Board

70. Metropolitan Museum of Art, Costume Institute Fashion Plates

73. Yale Center for British Art

74. Oxford, Bodleian Library, 13 θ 152, p. 210

77. National Gallery of Art, Washington, Gift of Addie Burr Clark 1946.9.237

78. Oxford, Bodleian Library, G.A. Yorks 4° 253, p. 140

80. Metropolitan Museum of Art, Costume Institute Fashion Plates

83. Yale Center for British Art, Paul Mellon Collection

84. Yale Center for British Art, Paul Mellon Collection

87. Yale Center for British Art, Paul Mellon Collection

88. Oxford, Bodleian Library, Vet. A5 b.82

91. Private Collection / Bridgeman Images

92. Oxford, Bodleian Library, John Johnson Collection, Indoor Games and Dancing folder (2)

95. Oxford, Bodleian Library, MS. Eng. e. 3764

96. National Gallery of Art, Washington, Andrew W. Mellon Collection, 940.1.11

99. J. Paul Getty Museum, Los Angeles. Digital image courtesy of the Getty's Open Content Program

101. Private Collection / The Stapleton Collection / Bridgeman Images

102. Yale Center for British Art, Paul Mellon Collection

105. © The British Library Board

107. Oxford, Bodleian Library, MS. Don. e. 7

108-9. Constable, *Wivenhoe Park, Essex*, 1816. National Gallery of Art, Washington, Widener Collection

110. Los Angeles County Museum of Art, Gift of Charles LeMaire (M.83.161.185)

## NOTES ON SOURCES

Quotations from the letters of Jane Austen are taken from the Brabourne Edition, 1884.

Punctuation and spellings have been modernized.

The quotation from *The Watsons* on p. 94 appears in MS. MA 1034, Morgan Library & Museum, New York.

Images from *The Repository of Arts, Literature, Commerce, Manufactures, Fashions, and Politics* (later *Repository of arts, literature fashions &c.*) by Rudolph Ackermann come from a variety of sources, given above. The periodical is referred to in its short title form: Ackermann's *Repository*.

First published in 2017 by the Bodleian Library
Broad Street, Oxford OX1 3BG

www.bodleianshop.co.uk

ISBN: 978 1 85124 464 5

Picture research by Leanda Shrimpton

Cover design by Dot Little at the Bodleian Library
Designed and typeset by Karin Fremer, in Bell MT
Printed and bound by Great Wall Printing Co. Ltd., Hong Kong on 157gsm matt art
British Library Catalogue in Publishing Data
A CIP record of this publication is available from the British Library